Road Trip: Famous Routes

The APPALACHIAN TRAIL

BY WALTER LAPLANTE

Gareth Stevens
PUBLISHING

Please visit our website, www.garethstevens.com. For a free color catalog of all our high-quality books, call toll free 1-800-542-2595 or fax 1-877-542-2596.

Library of Congress Cataloging-in-Publication Data

Names: LaPlante, Walter, author.
Title: The Appalachian Trail / Walter LaPlante.
Description: New York : Gareth Stevens Publishing, 2017. | Series: Road trip:
 famous routes | Includes index.
Identifiers: LCCN 2015051092 | ISBN 9781482446739 (pbk.) | ISBN 9781482449549 (library bound) | ISBN
9781482449433 (6 pack)
Subjects: LCSH: Hiking–Appalachian Trail–Juvenile literature. | Appalachian
 Trail–Juvenile literature.
Classification: LCC GV199.42.A68 L37 2017 | DDC 796.510974–dc23
LC record available at http://lccn.loc.gov/2015051092

First Edition

Published in 2017 by
Gareth Stevens Publishing
111 East 14th Street, Suite 349
New York, NY 10003

Designer: Andrea Davison-Bartolotta
Editor: Kristen Nelson

Photo credits: Cover, p. 1 (left) Jaminnbenji/Shutterstock.com; cover, p. 1 (right) Michael Marquand/Lonely Planet
Images/Getty Images; pp. 5 (background), 15 Dave Allen Photography/Shutterstock.com; pp. 5 (map), 9 (main)
AridOcean/Shutterstock.com; p. 7 Buyenlarge/Hulton Fine Art Collection/Getty Images; pp. 9 (inset), 18 Kelly
venDellen/Shutterstock.com; p. 10 MarkVanDykePhotography/Shutterstock.com; p. 11 Jon Bilous/Shutterstock.com;
p. 13 (main) Thomson200/Wikimedia Commons; p. 13 (inset) Sean Pavone/Shutterstock.com; p. 14 BackyardProduction/
iStock/Thinkstock; pp. 17 (both), 20 Portland Press Herald/Getty Images; p. 19 drewthehobbit/Shutterstock.com.

Printed in the United States of America

CPSIA compliance information: Batch #CS16GS: For further information contact Gareth Stevens, New York, New York at 1-800-542-2595.

Contents

Words in the glossary appear in **bold** type the first time they are used in the text.

Mountain Trail

Some of the best hiking, camping, and grand views are found along the Appalachian National Scenic Trail—and you might not need a long road trip to reach it. The trail crosses 14 states in the eastern United States, following the **crest** of the Appalachian Mountains. It also passes through six national parks and eight national forests!

The Appalachian Trail **stretches** from Mount Katahdin in Maine to Springer Mountain in Georgia. Between them are 2,190 miles (3,524 km) of adventure waiting for you!

Pit Stop

The longest stretch of trail is found in Virginia. It's 544 miles (875 km).

All About the
Appalachian Trail

where found: passes through Maine, New Hampshire, Vermont, Massachusetts, Connecticut, New York, New Jersey, Pennsylvania, Maryland, West Virginia, Virginia, Tennessee, North Carolina, and Georgia

year established: first section opened in 1923; became part of the National Trail System in 1968

length: 2,190 miles (3,524 km)

number of visitors yearly: 3 to 4 million people hike parts of the trail

wildlife along the trail: black bears, moose, coyotes, raccoons

plant life along the trail: azalea, dogwood, maple trees, pine trees

major attractions: Clingmans Dome, Harpers Ferry National Historical Park, many national parks

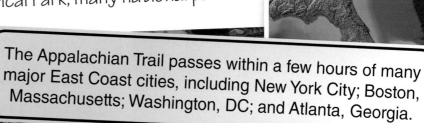

Appalachian Mountains

The Appalachian Trail passes within a few hours of many major East Coast cities, including New York City; Boston, Massachusetts; Washington, DC; and Atlanta, Georgia.

MacKaye's Dream

In 1921, a newspaper article started the creation of the Appalachian Trail. A former United States Forestry Service worker, Benton MacKaye, wrote that time spent in the great outdoors could help people enjoy their lives more. He wanted to build a trail between the highest point in the Northeast and the highest point in the Southeast with campsites along its length.

In 1925, MacKaye created the Appalachian Trail Conference to help work on his idea. By 1937, there was a footpath that led from Maine to Georgia.

Pit Stop

MacKaye was a **conservationist**. He once said: "How much more beautiful the surrounding would be, in every way, if men were not such fools."

This painting of Mount Katahdin shows that some people had already noticed the beauty of the Appalachian Mountain region, or area, and wanted to **preserve** it.

Complete!

World War II (1939–1945) slowed the **development** of the Appalachian Trail. Then, in 1968, the National Trails System Act passed, and the Appalachian Trail became the first national scenic trail.

The federal government and state governments were supposed to start buying the land around the trail so it could be **protected**. Much of this work fell to the Appalachian Trail Conference, which became the Appalachian Trail Conservancy in 2005. In 2014, all the land around the Appalachian Trail finally belonged to the government.

Pit Stop

The Pacific Crest National Scenic Trail was the second trail to be created under the 1968 act. It would make another great road trip!

Over the years, the Appalachian Trail's footpath has been moved in some places to take hikers to more scenic views and because of weather **disasters**. That's why the length of the trail may change from year to year.

Appalachian Trail

Appalachian Mountains

National Stops

A road trip to a section of the Appalachian Trail wouldn't be complete without a visit to a national park! Shenandoah National Park in Virginia is a great place to camp for a few days. You can either use one of their campgrounds or explore the park and camp in the **wilderness**.

Green Mountain National Forest in Vermont is a treat to visit in the fall. The mountains in the park are covered in trees that change to beautiful colors when it starts getting cooler.

Pit Stop

There are places to learn about history along the Appalachian Trail, too. Visit Harpers Ferry National Historical Park and Chesapeake & Ohio Canal National Historical Park!

Harpers Ferry National Historical Park

Skyline Drive Scenic Highway in Shenandoah National Park could be a great part of the road trip. It's a 105-mile (169 km) length of road that shows views of the Blue Ridge Mountains.

11

Clingmans Dome

The highest point along the Appalachian Trail is Clingmans Dome. At 6,643 feet (2,025 m) high, the mountain is also the tallest point in Tennessee! Clingmans Dome is in Great Smoky Mountains National Park. The Smokies are part of the Appalachian Mountains named for the blue fog that always seems to be around them.

Visitors can drive to the top of Clingmans Dome and hike a short way to an observation, or viewing, tower. From the tower, you can see across the Smokies if the weather is clear.

Pit Stop

Next to Great Smoky Mountains National Park in North Carolina is the Blue Ridge Parkway. You can drive along it for some great views!

Georgia's fourth-tallest mountain is a great stop along the Appalachian Trail. It's called Blood Mountain after battles fought there between the Cherokee and Creek peoples about 400 years ago.

Clingmans Dome observation tower

13

Wildlife Watcher

Though the Appalachian Trail was made for people to hike, it's also surrounded by **habitats** for many animals. Forests, streams, and meadows are just some of the habitats found along the trail.

If you're planning to use your hike on the Appalachian Trail to spot a lot of animals, you might be disappointed. Animals can smell people coming. Most will hide before you see them. Still, if you're very quiet, you may see moose, coyotes, deer, raccoons, and more.

Pit Stop

Hunters are allowed along all but about 600 miles (966 km) of the Appalachian Trail. Before you head out, find out if it's hunting season near where you're going. Always wear bright colors so you can be easily seen.

At certain times of the year, black bear warnings are issued in national parks near the trail to warn hikers that bears have been spotted.

Serious Hikes

You can take a hike on the Appalachian Trail for an afternoon or a few days!

- Mau-Har Loop, Virginia: To finish this 14-mile (22.5 km) hike, you'll camp overnight! Seeing tall waterfalls makes the challenging hike worth it.

- Anthony's Nose, New York: This part of the trail is just 2.2 miles (3.5 km), but steep. The Camp Smith Trail connected to it shows hikers New York City in the distance!

- Nantahala Mountains, North Carolina: Try a 29-mile (47 km) hike through **gorges** and valleys. Or take a short hike on one of the side trails!

Pit Stop

The 100-Mile Wilderness is a part of the Appalachian Trail in Maine where hikers will almost certainly be alone. It's a beautiful part of the trail, but should only be tried by skilled hikers.

The footpath can be narrow, steep, rocky, or smooth. Many websites can tell you what your hike will be like, allowing you to be prepared.

Taking on the Trail

Each year more than 1,000 people try to hike the *whole* Appalachian Trail! This takes about 5 to 7 months. These hikers often start at Springer Mountain around March or April and head north.

Hikers need to be fit so the long days of walking don't tire them too much. They also need to pack carefully. **Nonperishable** food that takes up little space, warm clothing, and good hiking shoes are just some of the important items they'll need.

Hiking the whole Appalachian Trail is called thru-hiking.

Pit Stop

There are **shelters** every 10 to 12 miles (16 to 19 km) on the trail, so hikers don't have to bring a tent.

"Leave No Trace"

Members of the Appalachian Trail Conservancy maintain the Appalachian Trail. They repair bridges and shelters and clear plant overgrowth. As they work, they talk to hikers and remind them of the most important rule of hiking the Appalachian Trail: Leave no trace.

Hikers should aim to leave the trail as they found it. That means never littering or harming any natural surroundings or trail buildings. All visitors can help keep this famous route in good condition for years to come!

Do you live near the Appalachian Trail? There might be a group you and your family can join in caring for the trail!

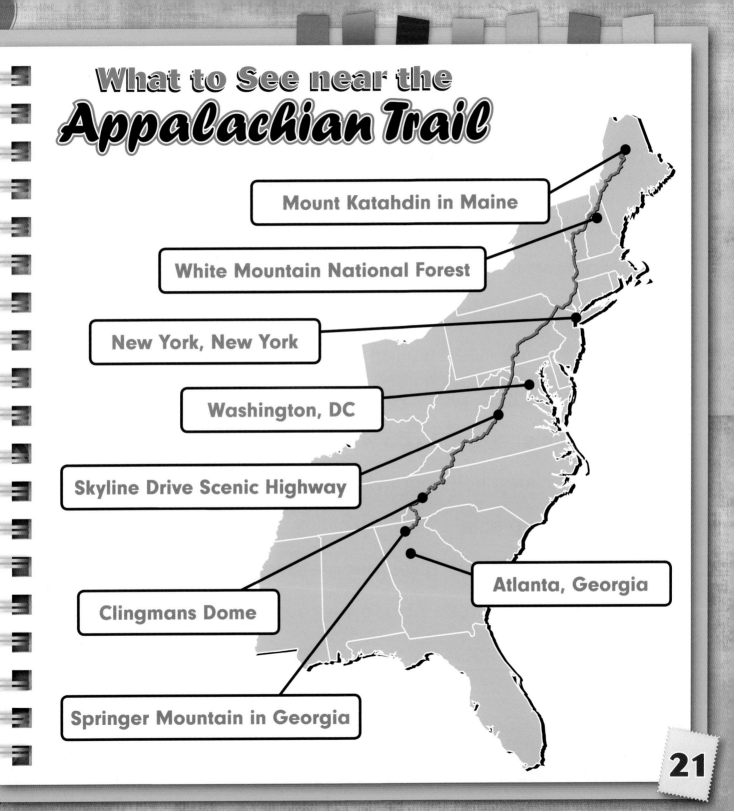

What to See near the Appalachian Trail

Mount Katahdin in Maine

White Mountain National Forest

New York, New York

Washington, DC

Skyline Drive Scenic Highway

Clingmans Dome

Atlanta, Georgia

Springer Mountain in Georgia

Glossary

conservationist: a person concerned with conservation, or the care of nature

crest: the top part of a mountain

development: the act or process of creating over time

disaster: an event that causes much suffering or loss

gorge: a narrow, steep-walled valley or part of a valley

habitat: the natural place where an animal or plant lives

nonperishable: having to do with the ability to not go bad

preserve: to keep in its original state

protect: to keep safe

shelter: a building that gives people cover

stretch: to reach across. Also, a piece or part of.

wilderness: land not developed by people

For More Information

Books

Aloian, Molly. *The Appalachians.* New York, NY: Crabtree Pub. Co., 2012.

Hengel, Katherine. *Cool Parks & Trails: Great Things to Do in the Great Outdoors.* Minneapolis, MN: ABDO Publishing, 2016.

Mitten, Ellen K. *Appalachian Region.* Vero Beach, FL: Rourke Educational Media, 2015.

Websites

Be a Junior Ranger
www.nps.gov/appa/learn/kidsyouth/beajuniorranger.htm
Find guides for kids who are hiking some parts of the Appalachian Trail.

10 Kid-Friendly Appalachian Trail Hikes
appalachiantrail.com/trail-mix/10-kid-friendly-appalachian-trail-hikes-from-amc/
If you want to hike parts of the Appalachian Trail, this website can help you find the right place to start!

Index